KEN PURKISS
50 PHOTOS

D1514319

Published by Kensworth Press
www.kensworthpress.com
e-mail: mail@kensworthpress.com

ISBN 978-0-9555707-0-4

Front cover: beagling in Hertfordshire.
Back cover: The New Forest Beagles.

Design and typesetting by Surfbird Design
www.surfbird-design.com

KEN PURKISS
50 PHOTOS

kensworth

Acknowledgements

We would like to thank everyone who has contributed to this book. Susanne Worsfold, Alistair Brown, Janet Kersnar, Serena McCall, Jane and Robert McWilliam and Joe Salem helped to choose the images most likely to appeal to a wide readership. Katherine and Harry Easterbrook, Jean Hancock and David Walker identified many of the people and animals in the photographs. Ken George and Edward Purkiss also helped with this and made valuable comments on the drafts. Robin Rogers provided up-to-date information on hunting, while Margaret, Roger and Simon Purkiss helped to edit the text. Fiona Carruthers, Alex Findlater, Lydia Kan, Kahéna Tlili, Yasuhiko Takayanagi and Andrea von Finckenstein provided feedback on the final drafts. We would also like to thank Rose Alexander for her advice on legal issues.

A Helpful Coincidence

I first got to know my co-author Robert Coggins as our tax advisor when I worked at Heidrick & Struggles, the executive search firm. A colleague and I worked with him again when we invested in a small software company.

One afternoon I met Robert in London and noticed the sports jacket he was wearing. "Do you go beagling?", I enquired, to which he replied, "Yes – are you Ken Purkiss's son?"

It turned out that Robert had known many of the people in Ken's photographs. His knowledge of hunting with foot packs enabled us to assemble the text of *50 Photos*. My family and I are very grateful for his contribution.

JP

www.johnpurkiss.com

Introduction

We have produced this book with two aims in mind. The first is to make Ken's photographs accessible to more people. The second is to raise funds for the charities that helped him cope with multiple sclerosis (MS) and provided treatment.

I am Ken's eldest son. A few months after he died, I looked through his boxes of prints and negatives. Most of the images I knew from books and magazines were there, together with some which are published here for the first time.

A short biography may be helpful. Ken was born in 1925 in Linslade, Buckinghamshire, a small town on the Grand Union Canal between London and Birmingham. His father Harry was a partner in a coach building business and his grandfather Edward was the landlord of The Goat, a pub across the road.

Ken attended The Cedars, a local grammar school, where he matriculated at the age of 16. His poor eyesight prevented him from joining the armed forces. Instead, he became a draughtsman at Foundry Equipment Ltd, where he designed depth charge racks for the Admiralty, among other things.

The photographs shown here were taken between 1946 and 1959. At the end of the war few people had access to high-quality camera equipment, much of which had previously come from Germany. Ken added industrial photography to his repertoire and his eye for composition is evident in his early work.

Ken loved the countryside and spent much of his spare time in the fields around Linslade. As a young man in the 1950s he became one of Britain's leading field sports photographers. He was a good friend of Jack Ivester Lloyd and Waddy Wadsworth, both keen beaglers and otter hunters. They later wrote books on hunting for which Ken provided some or all of the photographs.

This new book contains many photographs of beagling and foxhunting, both of which continue within the confines of the Hunting Act 2004. Otter hunting also features prominently. It ended in England and Wales in 1978.

Ken (far right) with friends including Waddy Wadsworth (third from left).

Ken followed the hounds on foot. Initially he used a Zeiss Ikonta camera, with 120 roll film which can produce frames of various sizes. Later he switched to a Contax, using 35mm film. Many of his pictures succeeded at the first attempt. They had to, since there were no motor drives to allow for multiple shots of the same subject. He developed and printed his own negatives.

Ken met our mother Margaret at a dance in Aylesbury. They married in 1959 and moved to Exeter in Devon, where Ken started a business with Waddy Wadsworth. Kensworth Publicity did not take off, and Ken later joined an office equipment company. Roger and I were born, and we moved back to

Jack Ivester Lloyd with Ken's dog, Mick, at the Ship Hotel, Linslade, winter 1955/1956.

Linslade, then Hertford, then Leicester, in the heart of foxhunting country. Roger and I, with our younger brother Simon, often did our best to follow the Fernie Hunt on foot, occasionally glimpsing them in the distance.

Already by 1960, when he was 35, Ken's physical coordination had deteriorated and he walked rather than ran. MS had perhaps already begun to take hold. As a child I did not understand why he could not catch – or play football. When he was 56 his condition was finally diagnosed and he was forced to retire. My parents and Simon then moved to Warminster in Wiltshire, a small town rather like Linslade in many respects.

The last years of his illness were often painful, both for Ken and for everyone close to him. Although he sometimes cried out when his limbs hurt, I never heard him bemoan his situation. He just seemed to accept it. Each time I was due to leave Warminster for London he insisted on coming with us to the station, even when that meant driving his buggy into the back of the van and waving goodbye from the station car park.

In the last years of his illness there were lucid moments, and some memorable one-liners. One day Ken was standing next to me on the platform at Warminster station. He leant on his Zimmer frame while we looked at two pigeons sitting on the gates to the scrap metal yard. Suddenly one pigeon jumped on the back of the other and they began flapping away excitedly. Ken nodded approvingly and said, "Never miss a chance".

Ken died in October 2005, two months short of his 80th birthday. Like many MS sufferers, Ken saw few people in his later years. However, his photographs remained well-known to those who possessed books by Jack Ivester Lloyd, Waddy Wadsworth and others.

50 Photos provides an opportunity to see Ken's work in a wider context. Some of these images challenge our assumptions. Others capture the beauty of the countryside or the joy of the moment. We hope you enjoy them too.

John Purkiss

THE PHOTOS

Ken's Mentors and Friends

Ken's school master, Ernie Samuel, was keen on hunting and encouraged his pupils to participate. Jack Ivester Lloyd and Waddy Wadsworth, perhaps southern England's two best-known figures in hunting circles, also happened to live nearby.

Jack was born in 1906, the son of the sporting artist, Tom Ivester Lloyd. He was brought up in Sherington near Newport Pagnell in Buckinghamshire. Jack went to sea at the age of fifteen. After a variety of other jobs he joined the Royal Naval Volunteer Reserve during the Second World War. Having become a Lieutenant-Commander, he was awarded the Distinguished Service Cross and was mentioned in despatches.

Jack was a keen naturalist and participated in minor field sports such as ratting, rabbiting and ferreting. He was also an enthusiastic beagler and otter hunter. On his return from the war he turned to journalism, regularly contributing articles on country matters and hunting to local newspapers and leading country periodicals. He also broadcast on radio for the BBC. Jack wrote over twenty books. These included *Come Hunting*, *Beaglers*, *Beagling*, *Rabbiting and Ferreting* (with Ernest Samuel) and *Hounds of Britain with Notes on their Quarry* as well as a number of children's books. He died in 1993.

1

Jack Ivester Lloyd examining an otter slide on the towpath at Linslade, Buckinghamshire.

2 Waddy Wadsworth goes for a swim at the Golden Lion at Ashburton, Devon, after a day's hunting.

3 Young Conservatives' day out on the Isle of Wight.

Waddy Wadsworth was the son of an Indian Railways official, who had retired to Bedford by the time Waddy was born in 1906. Before the Second World War, Waddy worked for the Ouse River Drainage Board. He then became a policeman, an intensive poultry farmer and a successful demolition contractor. The loss of his employees to the armed forces put an end to his business, leaving him in a reserved but unprofitable occupation. He spent the rest of the war salvaging motor vehicles. From then until retirement he worked in property, with a brief interlude when he and Ken set up Kensworth Publicity.

Like Jack Ivester Lloyd, Waddy was a keen naturalist and an enthusiastic beagler. After the war he took up otterhunting. He was Master or Joint Master of the Courtenay Tracy Otterhounds from 1953 to 1956 and of the North Bucks Beagles during the winter season from 1969 to 1970. In retirement he regularly contributed articles on country matters and hunting to the Western Morning News and leading country periodicals. Towards the end of his life he wrote two books – *A Sporting Life* and *Vive la Chasse*. Waddy died in 2000.

4

Waddy Wadsworth and Jack Ivester Lloyd with two border terriers.

5

Unvanning the South Herts Beagles.

Hunting in the 1950s

Ken initially photographed hunts and hunting people in Buckinghamshire, Bedfordshire and Hertfordshire. He later travelled to the Lake District, Wales and the West Country, mainly with packs which hunted on foot.

His photographs capture the essence of hunting, including the personalities and skills of particular hounds, and the relationship with the huntsman who brings out their potential. They also show the wide range of people who follow and participate in the sport. Some of them were mounted, though most in Ken's pictures were on foot: the gentry, plutocrats, shopkeepers, farmers, farm workers and young people.

Although some mounted packs still enjoyed prestige and pageantry, hunting was changing along with Britain's social structure. High rates of taxation on large fortunes meant that major landowners had little cash available to subsidise the local hunt, as they had traditionally.

Most of the packs featured in Ken's photographs had never enjoyed much prestige in any event. Many provincial beagle packs were tolerated rather than encouraged by local packs of foxhounds. Others, particularly in the Home Counties, enjoyed a certain degree of local recognition outside the hunting community. Such packs often had a higher proportion of professional and business people among their followers.

Otterhounds were the only packs to hunt during the summer. They were even less well-known outside the hunting community, since their followers were dispersed over the extensive areas in which they hunted.

Ken's photographs provide a reminder of how important foot packs were in the 1950s, providing a social life in isolated country districts during the winter.

6

The Pipewell Foot Beagles moving off from Geddington Cross, Northamptonshire. On the right in the foreground is Bill Hill, who completed 51 seasons as Master of Hounds.

Beagling

Beagling involves hunting hares on foot with a pack of hounds. As in foxhunting, the hounds hunt primarily by scent rather than sight. However, while foxhounds often cover a great deal of ground, followed by riders in their distinctive hunting coats, beagles may follow the movements of a hare on the same farm for three hours or more. This is because hares normally run in circles and return to home territory as soon as they can no longer see or hear the pack. For the last 25 years, the hare population in the British Isles has remained stable at between 800,000 and one million.

One of the attractions of beagling is watching the hounds puzzle out the hare's movements by following its scent. Beagling does not require deep pockets, the most expensive elements being travel and refreshments.

In Ken's day beagle packs were typically followed by self-employed shopkeepers, farmers and farm workers. Their numbers have since fallen, to be replaced by a wider range of people, including doctors, nurses, IT consultants, plumbers, builders, hairdressers and taxi drivers. There is also a greatly increased proportion of women and retired people. At weekends there are fewer followers than in the past, but they are drawn from an even wider social spectrum than during the week.

7
The South Herts Beagles in wintry conditions.

8

Hounds from the North Bucks Beagles. From left to right: Absinthe, Bellman, Daffodil and Bancroft.

9

A hare at full speed passes Mr Justice Sturge, Old Berkeley Beagles. He is taking cover to avoid diverting the hare.

10

Bryan Day with the New Forest Beagles.

11

The New Forest Beagles.

12

Ray and Edith Walker, landlord and landlady of the Ship Hotel, Linslade, Buckinghamshire.

13

Floods in Linslade, Buckinghamshire, circa 1947.

14

Ernie Fathers, a signwriter at Foundry Equipment Ltd.

15

Workers at Foundry Equipment Ltd. Clockwise from left to right: Bill Dowd, (unknown), G.Minall, T. Hignell, C. Scraggs, D. Reading, H, Baxendale, Bill Guess (kneeling).

16

Arthur Brown and his sister playing cricket.

17

Cumberland wrestling, which Ken attended during a hunt week in the Lake District.

Otter Hunting

Otter hunting began during the twelfth century. Freshwater fish were an important source of protein for those who lived away from the coast but still observed the Friday fast. Many fish were kept in small lakes, moats and monastery ponds. However, otters were found to be killing many of them, eating only the best bits. In 1174 Henry II appointed Sir Roger le Fol to the position of King's Otterer.

Otter hunting continued for over 800 years. From 1963 onwards, otter hunters noticed that the number of otters was declining. They adopted a policy of locating otters, but killing few of them. Many hunts stopped hunting otters altogether and either converted themselves into social clubs or began hunting mink and – for a short while – coypu. Despite having switched to other quarry, they used the same hounds and often retained the name otterhounds.

Post-mortems on otters revealed residues of pesticides such as aldrin and dieldrin, which had been widely used in the 1950s and seemed to have made the otters sterile. Their use was restricted from 1962 onwards, and ultimately banned. Otters became a protected species in England and Wales in 1978, in Scotland in 1981 and in Northern Ireland in 1985.

18

The Dartmoor Otterhounds watching the washing-up at Bow, Devon, in 1953.

There were many other factors in the decline of the otter population. These included the clearance and development of river banks, and the reduction in the food supply caused by acid rain. Nowadays 70% of otters found dead have been killed on the roads. Paradoxically, in West Somerset, Devon and Cornwall, where otter hunting continued for the longest period, there was hardly any decline in the otter population.

Otterhounds now pursue the descendants of American mink which began escaping from fur farms in the late 1950s, and have been blamed for driving water voles to the brink of extinction. The otters are making a comeback and are helping to drive out the mink.

19

Kennel huntsman with Captain Ronnie Wallace, Master of the Hawkstone Otterhounds, and a whipper-in. Ronnie was also a Master of Foxhounds for 58 consecutive seasons.

20
The Bucks Otterhounds crossing
rough water in the Lake District.

21

Mrs Moudy Robinson with her pet fox,
circa 1952.

22

Her brother-in-law, 'Doggy' Robinson (left),
and Harry Hardisty during a pause in a
day's hunting.

23

Mick and friend.

24

Cubs with otterhounds and a field secretary collecting money for the 'cap', to help finance the hunt.

25

Jack Ivester Lloyd otter hunting with a terrier.

26

The Courtenay Tracy Otterhounds moving off at Dorchester, 1954. Waddy Wadsworth is in the centre. Leigh Douse is on the right.

27

The Courtenay Tracy Otterhounds in Devon.

28

The Courtenay Tracy Otterhounds crossing a fisherman's bridge with Leigh Douse, the huntsman, in front and Waddy Wadsworth bringing up the rear.

29

Dick Nunn crossing the River Stour in Hampshire with the Courtenay Tracy Otterhounds.

30

The Courtenay Tracy Otterhounds with Lionel Douse, whipper-in, on the left and Leigh Douse, huntsman, on the right. The hound with the whiskers to the right of centre in the doorway is a purebred otterhound.

31

Jack Ivester Lloyd's dogs – a Jack Russell terrier and a dachshund named Rasper – in full flight.

32

Jack Absalom, kennel huntsman of the Bucks Otterhounds, on the flood plain of the River Ouse at Great Linford, Buckinghamshire, which is now part of Milton Keynes.

33

Peno Newman with the Eastern Counties Otterhounds near Cambridge.

34

The Eastern Counties Otterhounds swimming.

35

Colonel Michael Last with the Bucks Otterhounds 'marking' an otter at a hollow willow on the Great Ouse near Newport Pagnell, Buckinghamshire.

36

Followers of the Eastern Counties and the Bucks Otterhounds on a river bank. Third from left is Peter How, Master of the Hunt with the North Bucks Beagles.

37

Hounds from the Bucks Otterhounds scrambling up a riverbank. The one on the right is a retired foxhound.

38

Otterhounds dashing across a river.

39

The son of Murray Waite, an agricultural salesman, on a rabbiting expedition in the Chiltern Hills.

40

Badger digging at Wootton Bassett, Wiltshire. Waddy is lying in the foreground.

41

Ratting on the canal at Linslade,
Buckinghamshire, in 1949.

42

A ratting expedition at the Hills' Farm
in north Buckinghamshire. Left to
right: Elsie Hill, Philip Austin (whom
she later married), Jack Ivester Lloyd
and his wife Audrey. The car is an
Austin 16.

43

Cyril Sayell, a farmer and publican, with rhubarb at the Globe Inn, Linslade, Buckinghamshire.

44

Philip Austin, a whipper-in with the Bucks Otterhounds, releases a partridge from a trap probably intended for a mink or stoat.

45

Kennel Huntsman of the Equipage de St Raphaël, Bordeaux, France. He is holding a *trompe de chasse*, which is used for hunting deer, hare and boar.

46

Nubar Gulbenkian, the Armenian oil magnate, and his wife Marie, circa 1949. He was a keen follower of the Old Berkeley Beagles and the Whaddon Chase (foxhounds) for over 40 years. Nubar always wore an orchid in his lapel.

Fox Hunting

Foxes attack a wide range of livestock, including sheep and poultry, and are particularly effective at killing lambs. Packs of hounds were first formed specifically to hunt foxes after the restoration of King Charles II in 1660 when farmers and landowners set up their own private packs to hunt over each other's land. Virtually all fox hunts are now independent organisations, maintained and supported by subscription, rather than by one or two individuals acting as Master. As well as controlling foxes, foxhunts provide farmers and landowners with the valuable service of removing fallen livestock. The flesh and offal are used to feed the hounds. The rest is incinerated to prevent the spread of disease.

Fox hunting has always had a higher profile than beagling and otter hunting, partly because so many of the participants follow on horses. There are exceptions, such as in the Cumberland Fells, which are completely unsuitable for this. In many cases the master, kennel huntsman and whipper-in wear red hunting coats, often known as 'pink'.

Some of Ken's photographs feature the Whaddon Chase and the Old Berkeley hunts. Their followers included members of some of the richest families in England – the Rothschilds, Roseberys and Gulbenkians. However, a form of equality prevailed even among these hunts. Nubar Gulbenkian, for example, took special pride in performing the role of gateshutter. He and Lord Rosebery were popular among the foot followers and other supporters.

47

Autumn hunting at Mentmore Park, the estate of Lord Rosebery, in Buckinghamshire. Mrs Stoddart of Cheddington is accompanied by the groom and hunt secretary.

Photo 47 on the previous page shows autumn hunting – which begins early in the morning – on the estate of Lord Rosebery. By contrast, photo 48 shows the Lamerton Foxhounds, then a provincial farmers' pack operating on a shoestring budget. In addition to the mounted field, as many if not more subscribers followed on foot, on bicycles and by car.

Foxhunting continues in various forms, within the limits imposed by the Hunting Act 2004. A large number of hunt followers live in the cities, as do an increasing number of foxes, having no natural predators there.

There are currently 318 registered hound packs in England and Wales. 184 of these are foxhound packs. 72 are beagle packs and 20 are mink packs.

48

Frank Gerry, Huntsman of the Lamerton Foxhounds, cub hunting in Devon, 1954.

49

A farmer with a collie bitch, her puppies and a litter of fox cubs at Weedon, Buckinghamshire. They were brought up together and the fox cubs lived in the upholstery of a settee.

50

Mrs Rideout with her border terrier and pet fox.

The Wessex MS Centre

According to the MS Society, multiple sclerosis (MS) is the most common disabling neurological condition affecting young adults. Around 85,000 people in the UK have the disease, which results from damage to myelin, a protective sheath surrounding nerve fibres of the central nervous system. When myelin is damaged, it interferes with messages between the brain and other parts of the body, with symptoms which vary greatly from one day to another. They can include loss of balance, mobility, sight, sensation and speech. Swallowing, cognition and the immune system can also be affected. There is currently no cure.

The National Health Service offers limited treatment. The gap is partly filled by charities such as the Wessex MS Centre, in Warminster, which serves much of Avon, Hampshire, Somerset and Wiltshire. Treatments include physiotherapy, reflexology and chiropody. There is also a pressure chamber, shared with the local fire brigade, which provides hyperbaric oxygen therapy. This helps to reduce fatigue and accelerate the healing of skin ulcers. The Centre also provides counselling, advice and friendship.

The Wessex MS Centre is a registered charity, number 800851. Those who use it are asked for modest donations and also help with fund raising, if they are able. Many of them cannot work, nor can their carers. Those of us involved in producing *Ken Purkiss – 50 Photos* have donated our services and paid for the conversion of the negatives and prints into digital form. All profits from printing and selling this book are being donated to the Wessex MS Centre.

If you would like to make a donation, please contact:

Multiple Sclerosis Therapy Centre (Wessex) Ltd
Bradbury House
The Avenue
Warminster
Wiltshire BA12 0AB

Charity number 800851.

E-mail: manager@wessexms.co.uk
Telephone: +44 (0) 1985 217728

If you are a UK taxpayer, please ask the manager for a Gift Aid form. This will enable the Charity to reclaim the tax and increase the value of your donation by up to 66%.

Thank you for your support!

Robert Coggins, John Purkiss and Susanne Worsfold